INDUSTRIAL STEAM IN ACTION

ROGER SIVITER ARPS

GREAT BEAR PUBLISHING

0-6-0ST *No 4* pauses during shunting duties outside the weighbridge office at Birchenwood Gas & Coke Co. Ltd. at Kidsgrove in north Staffordshire. 26 July 1972. See also pictures on pages 38 to 41.

Above: On a fine autumn day – 23 October 1969 – 0-6-0ST *Littleton No 5* skirts the edge of Cannock Chase as it heads for Littleton Colliery with a load of empty wagons from Penkridge exchange sidings. See also pictures on pages 18 to 23.

Front Cover: On 10 April 1972 at Peckfield Colliery near Micklefield in the NCB North Yorkshire area, *No S100*, a Hudswell Clarke 0-6-0T (Works No 1822, built in 1949), propels a heavy load out of the colliery yard towards the spoil tip. See also picture on page 46.

Right: It is lunchtime at Preston Docks on Thursday 28 March 1968, and a pair of Bagnall outside cylindered saddle tank locomotives take a well earned rest before their afternoon's work begins. The front locomotive is *Enterprise* which was built in 1946, Works No 2840, and the rear locomotive *Energy* was also built in 1946, Works No 2838. This location was run by the Port of Preston Authority, and by the following year (1969) diesel traction had taken over, with one Bagnall 0-6-0ST *Courageous* (Works No 2892, built in 1948) being retained as a spare locomotive. *Hugh Ballantyne*

Introduction

I first became aware of industrial steam in 1966, not long after I had started to photograph BR steam. My good friend and fellow musician Ken Blocksidge, who also accompanied me on many railway trips, told me that the Austin Motor Company at Longbridge, Birmingham, had a fine fleet of steam locomotives that operated in the works area, as well as at the BR exchange sidings. As Ken also worked for Morris Commercial in Birmingham, which was by then part of the Austin Group, he was able to arrange a visit for us both (see pictures on pages 14 and 15).

It was a most enjoyable visit seeing their attractive locomotives, and I vowed that when steam finished on BR, which was only two years away, I would spend as much time as I could photographing the wide variety of steam at work in British industry. In doing this, I was helped enormously by the very informative booklets published by both the Industrial Railway Society and also by the Warwickshire Railway Society, both of which societies are still going as strongly as ever today.

At one time, there were many hundreds of industrial locations that employed steam locomotives, and so this book must be regarded as an overview of industrial steam at work. Thirty five different locations, from Cornwall and Kent up to Scotland, are covered, featuring breweries to collieries, with a wide variety of locomotives, the oldest having been built in 1873. On the last page is an index of locations featured in the book.

In compiling this work, I would like to thank Hugh Ballantyne and my wife Christina for much help and, last but not least, all the people who ran the industrial locations that I visited. I must say that in all my visits to the locations I was always given much assistance and shown great friendliness by the staff.

Please note that unless otherwise stated all pictures were taken by the author.

Roger Siviter
Evesham, 2005

© Roger Siviter 2005
Published by Great Bear Publishing
34 Shannon Way, Evesham WR11 3FF Tel: 01386 765134

£16.99

ISBN 0-9541150-5-8

Designed and printed by Ian Allan Ltd, Hersham, Surrey KT12 4RG

BIBLIOGRAPHY

INDUSTRIAL STEAM ALBUM, VOLUMES ONE and TWO
by M. J. FOX and G. D. KING. Publisher IAN ALLAN.

INDUSTRIAL RAILWAYS OF THE BRITISH ISLES, VOLUME ONE: STEAM
by KEVIN LANE. Publisher OPC.

Various booklets by the INDUSTRIAL RAILWAY SOCIETY and WARWICKSHIRE RAILWAY SOCIETY.

NORTHERN STEAM
published by the NORTH EASTERN LOCOMOTIVE PRESERVATION GROUP,
compiled by R. M. WHEELER & P. PROUD.

Bowne & Shaw Ltd. (later Tarmac Roadstone Holdings Ltd.) at Middle Peak Quarry, Wirksworth, Derbyshire, at the time that these two pictures were taken, on 23 February 1971, possessed what was one of the oldest (if not *the* oldest) steam locomotive at work in industrial use. *Holwell No 3*, an 0-4-0ST, was built by Black, Hawthorn & Co. Ltd. in 1873 (Works No 266).

The first scene on the (*left*) shows this fine looking vintage locomotive as it runs off the shed area after being serviced. At the rear can be seen the other 0-4-0ST *Uppingham* (see pictures on the following pages).

The second view *(above)* shows *Holwell No 3* shunting hopper wagons out of the BR exchange sidings. Note the red lining-out on the locomotive and motion, and also the fact that it is still working in its 98th year!

A further visit to Wirksworth Quarry on 14 April 1972 enabled me to photograph the other vintage steam locomotive at work in this scenic location, *Uppingham*, an 0-4-0ST built by Peckett & Sons Ltd. in 1912, Works No 1257.

The first picture *(top)* shows *Uppingham* as it shunts in the quarry yard, with the quarry in the background.

In the second scene *(above)*, we see the veteran locomotive as it heads for the quarry yard with loaded limestone wagons, and the final view *(right)* shows the attractively lined-out locomotive at work in the limestone quarry itself. Note the lime kilns, etc.

The branch line from Duffield (on the Derby to Chesterfield line) to Wirksworth closed to passenger traffic in 1947, but remained open until the 1980s to service the quarry. Happily, it is now in the process of being preserved.

Left: Our final view at Wirksworth Quarry was taken on 23 February 1971, and shows *Holwell No 3* storming out of the exchange sidings with empty wagons bound for the quarry.

Above: On 18 August 1975, 0-6-0ST *No 6* from Backworth locomotive shed shunts a heavy load of wagons in Eccles Colliery yard. (See overleaf.)

Backworth locomotive shed (NCB) was situated at Eccles Colliery on the B1322, a short distance from Backworth BR station, which was situated on the northerly route from Newcastle to Monkseaton and Whitley Bay. Backworth was the last steam worked shed in Northumberland, diesel traction taking over completely in 1976.

When I visited the system on 18 August 1975, two very smart looking Austerity type 0-6-0STs were still in use, *No 6* (built by Bagnall in 1944, Works No 2749) and *No 9* (built by Robert Stephenson & Hawthorns in 1943, Works No 7097).

The first picture *(top left)* shows *No 9* shunting near Eccles Colliery and later *(bottom left)* as it approaches Burradon Colliery, some two miles west of Backworth, with a loaded train from Eccles Colliery. Note the attractive looking wagons, and also the crossing gates.

The final scene *(above)* shows *No 6* in the NCB blue livery, as it shunts near Eccles Colliery.

Bickershaw Colliery, situated at Leigh just to the west of Manchester, had the distinction of being one of the last collieries to use steam; this lasted until 1984, albeit in a standby capacity.

Above: A visit on 21 June 1972 shows *Spitfire*, one of three Hunslet Austerity type 0-6-0STs, first of all leaving the colliery with a heavy load for the BR exchange sidings, and secondly *(top right)*, pausing near the colliery between shunting duties. This locomotive was built in 1955 (Works No 3831) and was fitted with a Giesl ejector.

The third picture *(bottom right)* was taken some eleven years later, on 14 April 1983, and shows standby locomotive Austerity type 0-6-0ST *No 7* (Hunslet) shunting the new type hopper wagons in the colliery yard. On the right is the locomotive shed, with the colliery's diesel locomotive outside.

Third photograph: Christina Siviter

I mentioned in the introduction a visit to the Austin Motor Co. at Longbridge in Birmingham. This occurred on the morning of Saturday 4 June 1966. By this date, as can be seen in the following pictures, they still had a fine fleet of steam locomotives, which were highly maintained and kept in immaculate condition.

Left: These two pictures show *Austin 1*, an 0-6-0ST built by Kitson in 1932, Works No 5459, first of all as it heads out of the works towards the BR sidings, situated just to the north of the old disused Longbridge station which served the works, and was part of the old MR Halesowen–Longbridge branch which closed in 1963. The lower scene shows *Austin 1* running through the old station on its return to the works. Note the ornate station lamp and the booking hall / office above the line, which is still there today. The station was also used to load the new cars onto the car flats for transportation to the docks, etc.

Right: *Austin 11* pausing during shunting work. This 0-6-0ST locomotive was built by Hunslet in 1936, Works No 1692.

Below: The final scene shows one of the powerful newer locomotives, *Victor*, which was built by W. G. Bagnall Ltd. of Stafford in 1951, Works No 2996. Note the Walschaerts valve gear and the "Austin" badge, and also the shape of the saddle tank, a characteristic of the later locomotives built by Bagnalls.

Another famous Birmingham firm allied to the motor trade which used steam locomotives was the Dunlop Rubber Co. Ltd. at Fort Dunlop, situated between Gravelly Hill and Castle Bromwich on the eastern side of the "Second City".

It was not easy to get into the "Fort" but once again through my musical connections – I was teaching a young man the trumpet, who was also a rep for Dunlops, who arranged a visit for me – I was able to see the steam in action. And only just in time, because not many months after my visit on 20 May 1969, not only had the steam been made redundant but most of the trackwork had been taken up.

The first view *(left)* shows *No 7*, an 0-4-0ST built by Peckett in 1951, Works No 2130, heading from the exchange sidings with a load of vans. Part of the famous "Fort" can be seen on the left hand side, and also several smart looking contemporary lorries.

The second view *(above)* shows an 0-4-0ST, built by Bagnall in 1941 (Works No 2648) and formerly known as *No 6*, undergoing a boiler test prior to resuming work on the system.

The final picture *(right)* shows *No 7* waiting while a wagon is rerailed by a splendid looking crane lorry.

I first became aware of the Littleton Colliery line on my many journeys up the M6 to the north west of England in order to photograph the remaining steam workings on BR. But it was not until the middle of 1968 that I first saw steam working on the line, for it was on one of those journeys that I spotted steam at work shunting the sidings, which lay just below the M6 motorway, near to the junction for the A5 to Cannock.

Littleton Colliery was situated in the village of Huntington, some two miles north of Cannock on the A34 road from Cannock to Stafford. The line from the colliery ran for approximately four miles in a westerly direction, crossing the edge of Cannock Chase and connecting up with the BR Wolverhampton to Stafford line, just south of Penkridge.

The first picture *(top)*, taken in the colliery's rear sidings, shows Hudswell Clarke 0-6-0ST *No 7* busy on shunting work. This locomotive was built in 1943, Works No 1752. 23 October 1969.

Below: The following day (24 October 1969) sees *No 7* at Boscomoor sidings (near the M6 motorway) pausing in its shunting duties, while *Littleton No 5* passes with a load from the colliery to the sidings at Penkridge. This handsome 0-6-0ST was built by Manning Wardle in 1922, Works No 2018. Note the ex-Southern Railway brake van.

A few weeks earlier than the previous two pictures, on 5 September 1969, and we see *Littleton No 5* at Penkridge on a permanent way train. In the background is the A449 Wolverhampton to Stafford road, beyond which is the BR Wolverhampton to Stafford line. Note the BR semaphore signals. Also, on the right hand side is (at this time) Littleton Colliery's only diesel locomotive, a Yorkshire Engine 0-6-0 DE built in 1959, Works No 2748.

A true winter's day at Littleton Colliery, and a stark reminder of how arduous industrial railway work could be. It is 19 December 1969, and the Hudswell Clarke 0-6-0ST *No 7* is seen *(left)* shunting loaded wagons at the rear of the colliery prior to the wagons being transported to the BR sidings at Penkridge.

Above: The second picture shows *No 7* in the front colliery yard, engaged in shunting duties, which must have been very cold work for the men shunting. Note the old wooden coal wagons.

On a personal note – at the time that I took these pictures, I was living in the northern suburbs of Birmingham at Great Barr, only a few miles from the Cannock area so, on a snowy day like this, I did not have too far to travel to get these winter scenes. Also, the pictures on pages 54 and 55 confirm that the winter of '69/'70 was certainly much harder weather than we get today.

Left: Reflection at Boscomoor sidings, as *Littleton No 5* does some gentle shunting before heading back to the colliery yard with a load of empties. 5 September 1969.

Right: Much to my regret, I did not start taking colour slides until a visit to Littleton Colliery, on 4 September 1969. This was one of the very first pictures that I took that day, and shows *Robert Nelson No 4*, an 0-6-0ST built by Hunslet in 1936, Works No 1800, shunting in the rear colliery yard. Note the mixture of wooden and metal wagons. A comparison with the picture on page 27 is also worthwhile.

Below: The final picture on this attractive colliery system shows *No 6*, an 0-6-0ST built by Robert Stephenson & Hawthorns in 1945, Works No 7292, as it leaves Penkridge and heads for Littleton Colliery on 3 April 1969. The ex-Southern Railway brake van *Littleton Colliery No 1* is shown to good effect, as is my 1967 Morris Mini-Minor!

Around half a mile east of Stourport station on the BR Shrewsbury to Hartlebury line (the old Severn Valley route) was a junction for a short branch line, about a mile in length, which ran south to Stourport Power Station. To work this line and inside the power station, the CEGB at one time used a fleet of three 0-4-0STs.

This evening shot was taken on 5 July 1972, and shows one of the saddle tanks *WA No 2* as it rests outside the neat looking locomotive shed after a day's shunting work. This locomotive was built by Peckett & Sons Ltd. in 1936, Works No 1893.

Coal traffic by rail to the location, which with the closure of the line from Bewdley to Stourport in 1970 had been from Hartlebury only, ceased in 1979, and this fine looking power station was demolished in the early 1980s.

An earlier picture of *WA No 2* was taken on 14 April 1969, and shows the 0-4-0ST at work at the power station, shunting laden wagons into the coal tippler. Note the stockpiles of coal in the foreground of the previous picture.

Above: A close up of *WA No 2* outside the locomotive shed on 26 November 1972.

Below: This final scene at Stourport Power Station was taken on 20 March 1972, and shows 0-4-0ST *Sir Thomas Royden*, built by Andrew Barclay in 1940 (Works No 2088) as it crosses over the Stourport to Worcester road (A4025) with a load of coal for the power station (just off the left of the picture) from the exchange sidings with BR, which were situated off the right hand side of the picture. The girder bridge was demolished in 1986, but the right side abuttment remains, as does the public house. The site of the old power station is now a housing estate.

R. B. Tennant Ltd. employed a small fleet of vertical boilered Sentinel steam locomotives at their Whifflet Foundry at Coatbridge, Lanarkshire. *Ranald*, which was built by Sentinel at their Shrewsbury works in 1957 (Works No 9627), poses for the camera in the works yard on Sunday 4 August 1975.

Some ten miles south east of Ayr on the Dalmellington branch line was situated the NCB Waterside system, which served the Pennyvenie and Minnivey collieries (in the south east) and the Danaskin coal preparation plant, some three and a half miles north west of the collieries.

On 5 August 1975, two of Waterside's fleet of five outside cylinder tank locomotives (all built by Andrew Barclay) *No 17*, an 0-6-0T built in 1913 (Works No 1338), and *No 10*, a "Pug" 0-4-0ST built in 1947 (Works No 2244), are seen shunting in the yard at Dunaskin. Note the lovely old wooden wagons.

These next two views, taken on 30 August 1973, show 0-6-0T *No 24*, built in 1953 (Works No 2335), as it pulls out of Minnivey Colliery and heads for Dunaskin washery. Note that the locomotive is fitted with a Giesl ejector.

Above: The spoil tip for the Waterside system was situated roughly halfway between the collieries and Dunaskin, and this first picture shows another Barclay "Pug" tank, *No 21*, silhouetted against a dramatic sky as it shunts on the tip on 30 August 1973. This 0-4-0ST was built in 1949 (Works No 2284).

Below: This second view, taken some two years later on 5 August 1975, shows *No 17* in action on the – by now – famous Waterside tip. In both pictures, note the low-sided wooden wagons coupled to the locomotives, which are used as supplementary coal tenders.

Above: This final view on the Waterside system shows 0-4-0ST *No 10* as it shunts wagons by the side of Dunaskin coal preparation plant. 5 August 1975.

This system, with its attractive fleet of locomotives and general activity, plus the pleasant Ayrshire scenery, made it a "must" for any enthusiast visiting Scotland. Sadly, the line closed in 1978.

Right: Just before the end of steam on BR in August 1968, I spent a holiday in the southern part of Cornwall, which of course by this time had not seen any regular main line steam activity for several years. However, much to my joy, I discovered that not only Falmouth Docks & Engineering Co, Ltd. had industrial steam still at work, but that this was also the case at the Port of Par, Ltd.

On 31 July 1968, *No 5*, a Hudswell Clarke 0-4-0ST of 1929 vintage (Works No 1632), is seen shunting at Falmouth Docks.

As with the previous picture, these next two scenes were also taken on 31 July 1968 and also from the grounds of Pendennis Castle, which afforded excellent views of the docks and the activity therein.

The first picture (above) is a close up of No 5 as it ambles through the docks with a petrol tank wagon.

The final scene shows a panoramic view of this busy Cornish dockyard, with *No 5* on shunting duties. Note the amount of shipping on display and the variety of cranes in use. In the background is the Roseland Peninsula.

Falmouth Docks had three locomotives on the system; one was kept as a spare and the other two each worked one week on and one week off.

A visit to the English China Clays (ECC) at Par Harbour on 8 August 1968 shows *Judy*, an 0-4-0ST built by Bagnall in 1937 (Works No 2572), shunting near the china clay drier. *Judy* was one of the two Bagnall 0-4-0STs used on the system, the other locomotive being *Alfred*, which was built in 1953 (Works No 3058). Note the reduced height of the locomotive (common to both engines) due to the 7' 6" loading gauge clearance on some of the bridges under which the locomotives worked.

Right: On 29 July 1968 at Port of Par *Judy* is seen leaving one of the sheds. Note the height of the van next to the locomotive.

Below: This final picture at Port of Par was taken on 8 August 1968, and shows *Judy* as it heads towards the BR exchange siding with a van train. This view once again illustrates the size of the locomotive against a standard BR van, and also shows the opening at the rear of the cab. The rail system at Port of Par closed in the late 1970s, however both locomotives were destined for preservation.

Birchenwood Gas & Coke Co. Ltd. at Kidsgrove in North Staffordshire was an interesting but a little run down industrial location which had four locomotives on its books, with normally two engines in steam daily and, at one time, pairs of locomotives working alternative weeks.

Left: I made three visits to this location in the summer of 1972, the first being on the 20 June when I photographed *No 5*, built by Peckett & Son in 1954 (Works No 2153), taking in water outside the locomotive shed.

Right: The second view, taken on 26 July 1972, shows *No 4*, a Bagnall 0-6-0ST built in 1944 (Works No 2680), reflected in one of the "ponds" found on the system.

Below: The third picture, taken on the previous day (25 July), shows the other locomotive at work on the system that week. The Peckett 0-6-0ST *No 5* is seen resting between shunting duties outside the weighbridge office. Behind the locomotive is part of the gas and coke works.

On 26 July 1962, *No 4* is seen shunting wagon loads of spoil at the Birchenwood Gas & Coke Co. at Kidsgrove.

One final note – the other locomotives that used to work on this North Staffordshire industrial system were *No 2*, an Avonside 0-6-0ST of 1897 vintage (Works No 1382), and *Alexander*, an 0-4-0ST built by Bagnall in 1922 (Works No 2107). Although I said earlier that pairs of engines at one time worked alternate weeks, by 1972, when I visited the location, the above mentioned engines were by then in the locomotive shed, out of use.

Cadley Hill Colliery, at Castle Gresley (just in Derbyshire) near Burton on Trent, like many collieries was set in a rural area. I paid several visits to this attractive system in the early/mid 1970s, for although there were only two steam locomotives on their books, several locomotives were transferred to Cadley from nearby collieries.

There was also a newly built engine shed and small workshop, and the locomotives were kept in nice condition, as witness this picture *(top left)*, taken on 21 November 1973, of 0-6-0ST *Empress*, built by Bagnall in 1953 (Works No 3061), as it pauses during shunting duties in the colliery yard. The rear of the loco shed/workshop can be seen on the right hand side of the picture.

I mentioned earlier the transferrence of locomotives, one such being 0-6-0ST *Progress*, seen here shunting near the exchange sidings on 15 December 1972 *(below left)*. This locomotive, which was built by Robert Stephenson & Hawthorns in 1946 (Works No 7298), had recently been transferred from Measham Colliery when that system went over to diesel traction.

Above: The picture shows the pride of the colliery, Hunslet 0-6-0ST *Cadley Hill No 1*, as it leaves the exchange sidings with empties for the colliery on 24 March 1972. (See also picture on back jacket.)

Above: This penultimate picture at Cadley Hill Colliery shows 0-6-0ST *Empress* as it enters the colliery yard with a load of empty wagons from the exchange sidings. 21 November 1973.

Right Top: The final picture at Cadley Hill Colliery, taken on 23 July 1974, shows *Cadley Hill No 1* leaving the exchange sidings for the colliery. In the background can be seen Drakelow Power Station.

Right Bottom: We leave the Midlands and head north to the vast Yorkshire coalfields, where in its heyday there were dozens of collieries with steam locomotives at work. The first one we look at is Maltby Main Colliery in the NCB South Yorkshire Area.

On 25 August 1967, veteran 0-6-0ST *Rothervale No 1*, built by the Yorkshire Engine Co. Ltd. in 1929 (Works No 2240) is seen getting up steam pressure, prior to commencing the day's work at the colliery.

Above: The front jacket picture of this book shows a scene at Peckfield Colliery in the North Yorkshire Area. On that same day, 10 April 1972, another locomotive was in steam and at work at this colliery system, *Primrose No 2*, a Hunslet 0-6-0ST, built in 1952 (Works No 3715). This attractive locomotive is seen returning to the colliery after a trip to the spoil tip. The colliery was situated on the south side of the York to Leeds main line (immediately west of Micklefield station), which can be clearly seen to the left of the locomotive.

Our next colliery in the North Yorkshire Area, Fryston, is also situated next to a main line, this time on the north side of the Castleford to York line, about three miles east of Castleford.

Top right: On 27 October 1971, *Fryston No 2*, an outside cylinder 0-6-0T built in 1955 by Hudswell Clarke (Works No 1883), is seen shunting loaded wagons in the colliery yard, overlooked by the wheelhouse, etc. In the foreground is the BR line, and just in front of the locomotive can be seen an industrial semaphore bracket signal, which controls the movement from the colliery onto the sidings by the main line which, as our second picture *(bottom right)* shows, was used for shunting purposes. This scene was taken on a bright spring day in 1972 (10 April) and shows *Fryston No 2* at work on the sidings next to the main line.

The next two pictures *(left and below)* were taken on a misty 5 April 1971 at Cadeby Main Colliery, Conisbrough, in the NCB South Yorkshire Area, and show *Harold No 20*, a Hudswell Clarke 0-6-0T, built in 1942 (Works No 1731), first of all pausing for a "blow up", and then shunting wagons against a typical colliery backdrop. This colliery also served Denaby Main Colliery.

Right: South Kirkby Colliery in the NCB Barnsley Area is our next location. On 10 April 1972, 0-6-0ST *Kinsley No 9*, built by Hunslet in 1939 (Works No 1954), is seen pausing during shunting duties outside the locomotive shed *(top)*, and later on shunting in the colliery yard *(bottom)*. This lower view also shows, on the left hand side, the fairly large engine shed, which at one time was home to as many as five steam locomotives. But by the date of this picture only *Kinsley* was in use, with a Yorkshire Engine 0-4-0ST, built in 1949 (Works No 2474), used as a standby locomotive.

This colliery was situated just to the east of the B6422, between Hemsworth and South Kirkby.

Left: Thorne Colliery, Moorends, in the NCB Doncaster Area closed in 1968 but these two views, taken on 1 May 1965, show two of the interesting and veteran locomotives at work on this system at the time.

The first picture *(top)* shows 0-6-0ST *No 6*, built by Hudswell Clarke in 1918 (Works No 1349), pausing during shunting duties.

The second scene shows *Hatfield 4*, an ex GWR 0-6-0T No 944, shunting near the spoil tip. This locomotive originally belonged to the Llanelly & Mynydd Mawr Railway (LMM) and was called *Great Mountain*. It was built by Avonside Engine Co. Ltd. in 1902 (Works No 1448).

Two pictures: Hugh Ballantyne

Above: We end this Yorkshire colliery section with a visit to Manvers Main Colliery and workshops at Wath-on-Dearne in the NCB South Yorkshire Area. When I visited this location on 2 April 1970, it still had as many as a dozen locomotives on its books, but although many were out of use at least two would be in steam.

No 48, a Hunslet 0-6-0ST, built in 1948 (Works No 3685), is seen taking water prior to re-commencing shunting work. Note the driver giving instructions to the fireman.

Left: Also in steam at Manvers Main on 2 April 1970 was *No 49* (formerly known as *Ted*); this was another WD Austerity Type 0-6-0ST, built by Hunslet in 1950 (Works No 3701). The locomotive is seen outside the modern looking weighbridge office, pausing between shunting duties.

Below: The final picture at Manvers Main (on 2 April 1970) shows *No 48* again, this time outside the large locomotive shed and workshop, its day's shunting work having been done.

Not long after these pictures were taken, the steam was replaced by diesel traction, mainly ex BR diesel locomotives, and by 1972 there was only one steam locomotive left on standby duty, *No 65*, once again a Hunslet 0-6-0ST, built in 1964 (Works No 3889).

We leave Yorkshire and head north east to Northumberland to Ashington, where Ashington Colliery locomotive shed had a large allocation of steam locomotives in order to work at the collieries in the area.

The first picture *(above)* taken on 1 June 1966, shows 0-6-0T *No 31*, built by Robert Stephenson & Hawthorns in 1950 (Works No 7609), as it heads south at Potland junction with a load of coal from Ellington Colliery to Ashington. On the extreme left can be seen Linton Colliery (which closed in 1968). Note the fine array of semaphore signals. Also, at this point the train is about to pass Potland junction signal box.

This second picture *(below)*, also taken on the Ashington system on 1 June 1966, shows another Robert Stephenson & Hawthorns locomotive, this time 0-6-0ST *No 43*, built in 1956 (Works No 7769), which is seen climbing past Newmoor on the NCB line to Ashington with a load of coal from Ellington Colliery. *(Both: Hugh Ballantyne)*

I mentioned earlier the snowy weather that we had in the Midlands during the winter of 1969-1970, and this is certainly borne out by these two pictures, taken at West Cannock Colliery at Hednesford on 7 January 1970.

The first scene *(above)* shows veteran 0-6-0ST *Topham*, built by Bagnall in 1922 (Works No 2193), as it shunts by the side of the Walsall to Rugeley BR line. Note the LNWR lower quadrant signal and the LNWR Hednesford signal box.

The second picture *(right),* taken later on, shows *Topham* pulling a string of empty wagons out of the colliery sidings near to the BR line. West Cannock Colliery is off the left hand side of the picture, and in the background is part of a snow-covered Cannock Chase.

At the time these pictures were taken, the Walsall to Rugeley line, apart from diversionary traffic, was freight only, but some years later it was opened again to regular passenger traffic.

Stewarts & Lloyds (Minerals) Ltd. operated around twenty quarries in Leicestershire, Lincolnshire, the County of Rutland and Northamptonshire. A lot of their quarries were situated in the vicinity of Corby, where their giant Iron & Steel Works was located. Many locomotives were confined to the works site, but the twenty or so locomotives that worked the many quarries in the area were stabled at the large Pen Green Depot *(see picture overleaf)*.

The first picture, taken on 14 September 1965, shows *No 53*, built by Robert Stephenson & Hawthorns in 1941 (Works No 7030), as it crosses Gretton Brook Road on the S&L "main line" with a load of internal use wagons from Brookfield Sidings bound for the Corby Works.

(*Hugh Ballantyne*)

Above: This next picture shows Pen Green Shed at Corby, which was opened in 1954, with eight roads to hold up to forty engines. On shed on the evening of 14 September 1965 are five 0-6-0STs, all built by Robert Stephenson & Hawthorns. From left to right they are *No 56* (7667/50), *No 53* (7030/41), *No 63* (7761/54), *No 57* (7668/50) and *No 62* (7673/50). What a wonderful sight!

Below: An interesting scene on the S&L system at Brookfield Sidings, just north of Corby. A Hudswell Clarke 0-6-0ST *No 39 Rhos*, built in 1918 (Works No 1308), is seen in charge of a permanent way train. Note the smart looking vans. 14 September 1965.

(Both: Hugh Ballantyne)

Above: Glendon Quarries near Kettering, Northants, were also owned by Stewarts & Lloyds, and three locomotives were allocated there to work the system. On 15 September 1965, two of the three locomotives used are seen at Glendon East, pausing between shunting duties. On the left is *Carmarthen*, a Kitson 0-6-0ST, built in 1936 (Works No 5478), and on the right is *Caerphilly*, another Kitson 0-6-0ST, built in 1936 (Works No 5477). The third engine (not shown) was *No 80*, a Hunslet 0-6-0ST (Works No 2417), built in 1941. In the background is an Austin A35. This brings back memories to me, being only the second type of car that I bought, in 1963, the first (in 1957) being a 1935 Morris Eight.

Below: Our final picture on the many quarry systems of Stewarts & Lloyds was taken at Wellingborough Quarries, Northants. This metre gauge system was thought at the time to be the only one in the country. This picture was taken at the exchange point, Wellingborough, and shows skips of ore being unloaded. The locomotive in charge is *No 87*, one of three 0-6-0STs, built by Peckett & Sons, Ltd. and used on this system. This engine was built in 1942 (Works No 2029). 15 September 1965.

(Both: Hugh Ballantyne)

Top Left: Another company with quarries in Northamptonshire was the South Durham Iron & Steel Co. Ltd. with both their Irchester Quarries and Storefield Quarries using steam locomotives until the closure of the former in 1969 and the latter in the early 1970s.

On 14 September 1965, (by then) the oldest locomotive on either system, having been built in 1905, Storefield's *No 11* is seen shunting iron ore tipplers by the BR exchange sidings at Storefield, situated by the Midland main line from St Pancras to Nottingham. This veteran 0-4-0ST was built by Andrew Barclay (Works No 1047).

Bottom Left: Although at one time fairly common overseas, especially in South Africa, only four Beyer Garratt locomotives have worked on the British industrial systems, the last one being at the NCB Baddesley Colliery near Atherstone in Warwickshire. *William Francis*, 0-4-4-0G built by Beyer Peacock in 1937 (Works No 6841) is seen, now sadly out of use, outside Baddesley Colliery shed on 22 April 1967. At the time it was awaiting transfer to Canada for preservation.

I well remember visiting this location on the 15 May 1966 in order to see and get pictures of this rare locomotive in action, but on arrival at the colliery I was told that the engine had just been taken out of service and was locked away in the locomotive shed, viewable only through a side window. So I suspect that Hugh Ballantyne was lucky on this occasion even to see it outside the shed.

Of the other three Garrett type locomotives which worked in British industry, one was at Sneyd Colliery at Burslem, and the other two were to be found in South Wales.

Above: Also photographed on 22 April 1967, at Arley Colliery just north of Coventry, was an attractive looking Avonside 0-6-0ST *Joan*, caught by the camera as it shunts the older type of wooden coal wagons in the colliery yard.

As I said, this locomotive was built by the Avonside Engine Co. Ltd. in 1932 (Works No 2048). After closure of Arley Colliery in March 1968, the following September saw the transfer of *Joan* to Newdigate Colliery at Bedworth, both collieries being in the NCB South Midlands Area, which at the time covered Derbyshire, Leicestershire and Warwickshire. *(All: Hugh Ballantyne)*

Bowaters Paper Mills at Sittingbourne in Kent used two gauges, standard gauge between the mill at Kemsley and the BR Sheerness branch near Ridham, and the 2ft 6in gauge between the Sittingbourne works and Ridham Dock. These four pictures *(two overleaf)* of the system show work on the narrow gauge. When I visited Bowaters on 13 August 1969, steam on the standard gauge had finished, but the narrow gauge lasted a few more weeks, finishing on the 4 October 1969, when the NG system was leased to the Locomotive Club of Great Britain (LCGB), and was then known as the Sittingbourne & Kemsley Railway.

Top: shows 0-4-2ST *Premier*, built by Kerr Stuart in 1905 (Works No 886) as it crosses the viaduct which runs over the roads and Milton Creek at the south end of the system. The locomotive is running light towards the works. This locomotive was rebuilt in 1912.

Above: shows 0-6-2ST *Conqueror*, built by Bagnall in 1922 (Works No 2192), as it pauses in Ridham Dock during shunting duties. Note the spark arresting chimney (and also on *Premier* in the top picture).

Above: A short time after the previous picture, and we see *Conqueror* again as it leaves the Ridham Dock area and heads for the Sittingbourne factory with a train of empty wagons. Above the train is part of the aerial ropeway which ran between Ridham Dock and Kemsley Mill and carried logs for pulping. Kemsley Mill was situated roughly halfway between Ridham Dock and Bowaters Sittingbourne Mill and factory.

Left: The Bowaters narrow gauge system possessed a fireless locomotive *Unique* a 2-4-0F built in 1923 by Bagnall (Works No 2216). We see *Unique* as it shunts near Kemsley Mill, surrounded by mountains of paper.

Another feature of this fine industrial system were the special internal passenger trains run for Bowaters workers.

One final note; in its heyday, this narrow gauge railway had eleven locomotives on its books, with up to seven locomotives in steam daily, working 24 hours each day.

We leave the south east of England and travel north westwards to Haig Colliery at Whitehaven in Cumberland.

On the early evening of Thursday 30 August 1973, two Hunslet built Austerity Type 0-6-0STs were to be seen working at Haig Colliery. The first view *(top)* shows on the left *Repulse*, built in 1950 (Works No 3698), pausing during shunting work, whilst approaching the colliery with a load of coal from the washery at Ladysmith Coal Preparation Plant is unnamed 0-6-0ST, built around 1950 (Works No 3886). After arrival at the colliery, the wagons of washed coal are then lowered by rope down to Whitehaven Docks. In the second picture *(above)*, taken earlier in the afternoon, we see *No 3886* hard at work in the colliery yard.

Right: The brewers Bass, Ratcliff & Gretton, Ltd. operated an attractive industrial railway at their Burton on Trent brewery, the network covering some sixteen miles, plus some integrated mileage over the BR system. As well as the Bass locomotives, which were painted red, their associated company Worthington & Co. Ltd. also used the system, their locomotives being painted in a dark blue livery.

A visit to this splendid system on 4 June 1963 shows *(top)* 0-4-0ST *No 2*, built by Neilson Reid in 1900 (Works No 5760), and *(bottom)* 0-4-0ST *No 16*. This engine was built by W. G. Bagnall in 1923 (Works No 2108), and was originally numbered *Worthington No 5*, but was renumbered circa 1961 when the two companies amalgamated. Both are pictured outside the Bass Railway locomotive shed. These two pictures well display the distinctive liveries of the two famous brewery companies.

Until the closure of this system in the mid 1960s, Burton on Trent was famous (or infamous!) for the number of its level crossings. I know from personal experience!

(Both: Hugh Ballantyne)

Top and Above: These two views of Haig Colliery, also taken on the evening of 30 August 1973, show *(top)* Repulse shunting in the colliery yard, and earlier *(bottom)* pausing outside the weighbridge office, which seems to be perched on the cliffs, beyond which is the Irish Sea. (See also picture on page 80.)

We now concentrate on the South Wales area, where industrial steam locomotives (apart from stand-by duty) remained active until 1979/1980.

The first picture *(top left)* was taken at Talywain locomotive shed near Pontypool on 18 December 1972, and shows *Islwyn*, an 0-6-0ST taking a break after working at Talywain yard. This locomotive was built by Andrew Barclay in 1952 (Works No 2332).

This shed, which at one time had four locomotives on its books, also served the nearby Blaenserchan Colliery.

Bottom Left: Moving westwards into Glamorgan, we see this 0-4-0 fireless locomotive at the British Resin Products, Ltd. works at Sully near Barry. This locomotive was built by Andrew Barclay in 1948 (Works No 2238). This company was part of BP Chemicals (UK) Ltd. At the time, this was the only locomotive on this site and was in steam 6 days a week. *(Hugh Ballantyne)*

Above: At one time, Pontardulais shed (West Glamorgan) which served Graig Merthyr Colliery had an allocation of five steam locomotives, including a Sentinal. This would have been in the 1960s, but a visit to Pontardulais shed on 30 March 1978 produced only one locomotive in steam, this 0-6-0ST, which was built by Bagnall in 1944 (Works No 2758). Also seen at this location on the same day, but not in steam, was *Norma*, a Hunslet 0-6-0ST which was built in 1952 (Works No 3770). This locomotive was originally shedded at Maesteg Deep locomotive shed, which served the various collieries in the Maesteg Area. Graig Merthyr Colliery and the line finished on 23 June 1978, just weeks after this picture was taken.

(Hugh Ballantyne)

Mountain Ash Colliery and locomotive shed (and also workshops) in the NCB's South Western Division, Aberdare Area, was certainly in the 1970s one of the main systems on which to see a variety of industrial steam at work, and so it attracted enthusiasts from far and wide to this "Holy Grail" of Steam. The engine shed, which was home to up to six locomotives at a time, served the local colliery, Deep Duffryn Washery and, just north of Mountain Ash, Aberaman Phurnacite Plant. And so, with that preamble, I make no excuse for using several pictures of this now historic industrial mining area.

This first picture *(top)* was taken at Mountain Ash shed on the morning of 25 October 1972, and shows *(left to right)* 0-6-0ST *No 8* and *Llantanam Abbey*, an outside cylindered 0-6-0ST built by Andrew Barclay in 1939 (Works No 2074), behind which is 0-6-0ST *Sir John* – see following picture. This was a typical early morning scene with the locomotives being prepared for the day's work.

The second view *(bottom)*, taken near the shed a few weeks later on 18 December 1972, shows a close-up of *Sir John*. This famous locomotive was built by Avonside in 1914 (Works No 1680), and rebuilt by the same firm in 1929. In front of *Sir John* is *Llantanam Abbey*.

Top: On 2 January 1973 *No 1*, a Hudswell Clarke 0-6-0ST, leaves Mountain Ash yard with a load for the phurnacite plant at Aberaman. This locomotive, whose looks belie its age, was built in 1955 (Works No 1885).

The chapel and rows of houses stretching up the valley all add to this quintessentially South Wales colliery scene.

Below: Another of Mountain Ash's fleet of locomotives was *Sir Gomer*, seen here shunting in the shed yard on 8 May 1974. This 0-6-0ST was built by Peckett & Sons, Ltd. in 1932 (Works No 1859).

This panoramic view (taken with a 135mm lens) shows Deep Duffryn Colliery and washery on the afternoon of Thursday 25 October 1972, with the stalwart of the Mountain Ash system *No 8* preparing to hook onto another load of coal and shunt it to the washery. This 0-6-0ST was originally built by Robert Stephenson & Hawthorns in 1944 (Works No 7139) but rebuilt by the Hunslet Engine Co. Ltd. in 1961 (Works No 3880). On the left hand side is the former Taff Vale Railway line to Aberdare, which is now the main BR line in the area, whilst off the right hand side of the picture is the ex GWR line to Aberaman and on to Aberdare, which ran past the locomotive shed, and was at this time only used by colliery traffic. *(See picture on following page.)*

Above: This view, looking towards Mountain Ash locomotive shed and the NCB workshops, beyond which is the colliery, was taken on 25 October 1972. *No 8* is seen propelling loaded wagons on the ex GWR line to the phurnacite works at Aberaman, the train having just reversed into the locomotive yard from Deep Duffryn Washery. In the left background can be seen the remains of the old GWR station, still with a canopy, but by now the track has been lifted. This line originally ran from Pontypool Road to Aberdare and on to Neath.

Top Right: 0-6-0ST *No 8* again, this time shunting near the phurnacite works at Aberaman with another load of coal-dust waste from Mountain Ash. 12 March 1973.

Bottom Right: This side view of the elegant 0-6-0ST *Sir John*, shunting near Mountain Ash locomotive shed on 12 March 1973, was taken from the southbound platform of the old GWR station, and shows in the foreground the remains of the northbound platform.

Left: Whenever I have shown this picture at shows, etc. I usually preface it with the remark "This is what happens to you at Mountain Ash when you don't get permission to photograph" – which usually raises a laugh or two. But of course in reality, on my visits I was made more than welcome, as I was at all the locations in this book.

Hudswell Clarke 0-6-0ST *No 1* is photographed from inside the old GWR station as it pauses during shunting duties. 12 March 1973.

Below: On the same day as the above picture, *Sir John* is seen shunting near the locomotive shed. The inscription on the smoke box door reads "1913 - 1973, 60 years old and still going". In actual fact, the locomotive was originally built in 1914 and was still to be seen, looking in fairly good order, the following year (1974) in the locomotive depot.

Top Right: On 26 October 1972, *No 8* crosses the Afon Cynon with a heavy load of wagons for Deep Duffryn Washery. On the right hand side can be seen the ex GWR line to Aberaman (for the phurnacite works). On the left hand side through the smoke and mist can be seen the washery.

Bottom Right: Our final picture at Mountain Ash was taken on my last visit to this fascinating location, on Saturday 20 October 1979. On this day, a special train had been organised by the Monmouthshire Railway Society – the "Deep Duffryn Diddler" – from Newport to Mountain Ash for a steam hauled trip in open wagons on the NCB system, hauled by 0-6-0ST *No 8*. As well as *No 8*, 0-6-0ST *Llantanam Abbey* was also in steam, and is seen here near the locomotive shed. Also on display that day (but not in steam) was Peckett 0-6-0ST *Sir Gomer*.

Above: When the first standard gauge preserved lines started to operate in the 1960s and early 1970s, there were many ex industrial locomotives to be found at work on them. Sometimes these activities would be confined to shunting work and brake van trips, etc. but the more powerful engines were often to be seen on passenger work. This was certainly the case on the North Yorkshire Moors Railway (NYMR) in the early days, and is illustrated here with a picture taken on 28 August 1972 *(top)* of ex Lambton Railway 0-6-2T *No 29* climbing up to Ellerbeck with a train from Goathland. The location is just below Fylingdales Early Warning Station. This powerful locomotive was built by Kitson in 1904 (Works No 4263) and was based at the famous NCB Philadelphia locomotive shed. It used to work 24-wagon coal trains between Houghton Colliery and Sunderland Docks, and also worked around the Lambton Coking Plant.

Left: This view, taken at Bridgnorth yard on the Severn Valley Railway (SVR) on 23 May 1970, shows the more diminutive 0-6-0T *No 686*, pausing between shunting duties. At the rear is former GWR diesel railcar *No 22*. This attractive ex industrial locomotive was built by Hunslet in 1898 for the Manchester Ship Canal Railway, and was originally named *Sir John*. In the 1960s it was purchased by ICI for work at their Dyestuffs Division Works at Blackley, where it was repainted in a red livery and renamed *The Lady Armaghdale*. In 1969 it was offered for preservation, and purchased by the Warwickshire Industrial Locomotive Preservation Group and transported to Bridgnorth in July 1969.

Nowadays, industrial steam is not only to be seen on preserved lines, but occasionally it is featured on special charter events, where steam locomotives are transported to industrial locations such as coal mines, ports and factories. One such occasion was on 21 March 1999, when industrial locomotives from the Foxfield Steam Railway at Blythe Bridge, Stoke on Trent, were taken to the Shelton Steel Works at Etruria, Stoke on Trent, in order to recreate life-like industrial steam workings from the past.

The first picture *(above)* shows 0-4-0ST *Hawarden*, built by W. G. Bagnall, Ltd. in 1940 (Works No 2623), shunting in the billet mill.

The second view *(below)* shows a Dübs built crane tank, not in steam but posing for pictures. This 0-4-0CT was built in 1901 (Works No 4101) and, together with *Hawarden*, spent its working life at the Shelton Iron & Steel Co. Both locomotives were preserved at the Foxfield Steam Railway. *(Both: Hugh Ballantyne)*

INDEX

The sun sets over the Irish Sea as Hunslet 0-6-0ST (Works No 3886) performs its last shunting duties of the day at Haig Colliery, Whitehaven, on 30 August 1973.